WITHDRAWN

Evangeline Parish Library
916 West Main
Ville Platte, LA 70586

D1287486

VAMOS A AGRUPAR POR...
SORT IT OUT!

COLORES
Sort It by COLOR

By Emmett Alexander
Traducido por Eida de la Vega

Gareth Stevens
PUBLISHING

conceptos
básicos

Agrupar significa juntar cosas que son parecidas. Puedes agrupar por colores.

Sorting means putting things that are alike together. You can sort by color.

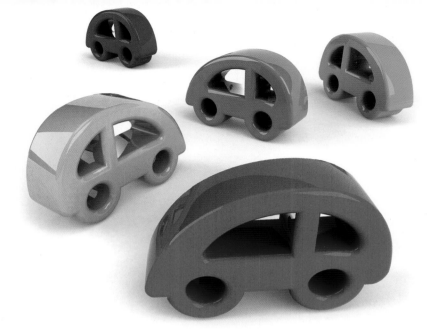

Estos juguetes son
de diferentes colores.

These toys are
different colors.

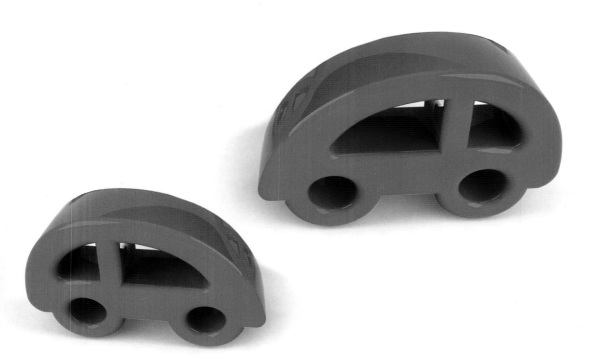

Estos juguetes son rojos.

These toys are red.

Estos bloques son
de diferentes colores.

These blocks
are different colors.

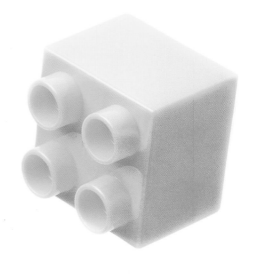

Estos bloques
son amarillos.

These blocks are yellow.

Estos peces son
de diferentes colores.

These fish are
different colors.

Estos peces
son anaranjados.

These fish are orange.

Estas verduras son
de diferentes colores.

These vegetables are
different colors.

Estas verduras
son verdes.

These vegetables
are green.

Estas camisas son
de diferentes colores.

These shirts are
different colors.

Estas camisas
son azules.

These shirts are blue.

Estas flores son
de diferentes colores.

These flowers are
different colors.

Estas flores son moradas.

These flowers are purple.

Estos crayones son
de diferentes colores.

These crayons are
different colors.

Estos crayones
son negros.

These crayons are black.

17

Estos libros son
de diferentes colores.

These books are
different colors.

Estos libros
son marrones.

These books are brown.

Estos conejos son
de diferentes colores.

- -

These rabbits are
different colors.

Estos conejos
son blancos.

These rabbits are white.

Una caja de bolas
está mezclada. ¿Cómo
agruparías estas bolas?

One box of balls is
mixed up. How would
you sort these balls?

23

Please visit our website, www.garethstevens.com. For a free color catalog of all our high-quality books, call toll free 1-800-542-2595 or fax 1-877-542-2596.

Library of Congress Cataloging-in-Publication Data

Alexander, Emmett.
Sort it by color = Colores / by Emmett Alexander.
p. cm. — (Sort it out! = Vamos a agrupar por...)
Parallel title: Vamos a agrupar por...
In English and Spanish.
Includes index.
ISBN 978-1-4824-3215-2 (library binding)
1. Group theory — Juvenile literature. 2. Colors — Juvenile literature. I. Title.
QA174.5 A449 2016
512.2—d23

First Edition

Published in 2016 by
Gareth Stevens Publishing
111 East 14th Street, Suite 349
New York, NY 10003

Copyright © 2016 Gareth Stevens Publishing

Designer: Sarah Liddell
Editor: Therese Shea
Spanish Translation: Eida de la Vega

Photo credits: Cover, p. 1 (polka dots) Victoria Kalinina/Shutterstock.com; cover, pp. 1 (gumballs), 23 Jenn Huls/Shutterstock.com; p. 3 Julie Vader/Shutterstock.com; pp. 4, 5 Julien Tromeur/ Shutterstock.com; p. 6 Nenov Brothers Images/Shutterstock.com; p. 7 tehcheesiong/Shutterstock.com; pp. 8, 9 Kietr/Shutterstock.com; p. 10 Serg64/Shutterstock.com; p. 11 Aprilphoto/Shutterstock.com; p. 12 GoodMood Photo/Shutterstock.com; p. 13 Apollofoto/Shutterstock.com; p. 14 Sascha Burkard/ Shutterstock.com; p. 15 Bildagentur Zoonar GmbH/Shutterstock.com; p. 16 Stephanie Frey/ Shutterstock.com; p. 17 Steve Gorton/Dorling Kindersley/Getty Images; p. 18 Quang Ho/ Shutterstock.com; p. 19 Brocreative/Shutterstock.com; p. 20 (colored rabbits) JIANG HONGYAN/ Shutterstock.com; p. 20 (white rabbit) camelia/Shutterstock.com; p. 21 (left) Eric Isselee/ Shutterstock.com; p. 21 (center) panbazil/Shutterstock.com; p. 21 (right) Iakov Filimonov/ Shutterstock.com.

All rights reserved. No part of this book may be reproduced in any form without permission in writing from the publisher, except by a reviewer.

Printed in the United States of America

CPSIA compliance information: Batch #CS15GS: For further information contact Gareth Stevens, New York, New York at 1-800-542-2595.